Street culture

ROCKPORT

First published in 2011 in the USA by
Rockport Publishers, a member of
Quayside Publishing Group
100 Cummings Center / 406-L
Beverly, Massachusetts 01915
USA
Phone: 987-282-9590
Fax: 978-283-2742
www.rockpub.com

Illustrations for Templates: Curl, Miwa Hirose, Yuki Kobayashi
Illustrations for Components: RYOKEN
Illustrations for Examples In Use: Andrew Pothecary (forbiddencolour)
Art Direction: Katsuya Moriizumi
Design: Andrew Pothecary (forbiddencolour)
Translation: Alma Reyes (ricorico)
Editing: Rico Komanoya (ricorico)

Production: ricorico

ISBN-13: 978-1-59253-666-5
ISBN-10: 1-59253-666-2

10 9 8 7 6 5 4 3 2 1

Printed in China

Street
culture

by ricorico

CONTENTS

HOW TO USE THIS BOOK
AND THE CD-ROM

This volume is a collection of usable artworks for designers and artists that features hundreds of popular and thematic subjects. It is designed to highlight the following categories:

Templates: *These are designed to be used as is, or to be manipulated, edited, and/or modified as preferred, for your personal and professional use. This chapter lies in the middle section of the book, and shows one item per page in order for you to see its details.*

Examples of Applied Templates: *In the following page, and before the Templates chapter begins, there are seventeen variations of examples of the applied templates illustrated in this chapter. From printed materials to interior decoration items, you can see how effectively the entire template drawing or a part of it can be rendered.*

Components: *All templates are made of multiple components introduced in this chapter. These components can be used as single or combined items, or joined with other components from other templates, to create your own unique and original artworks. The file numbers of the components correspond to the page number of the template illustrations.*

CD-ROM: *All the original files for the templates and components are digitally archived both in JPEG and in Adobe Illustrator vector files in the CD-ROM that is attached at the end of the book.*

EXAMPLES

Album

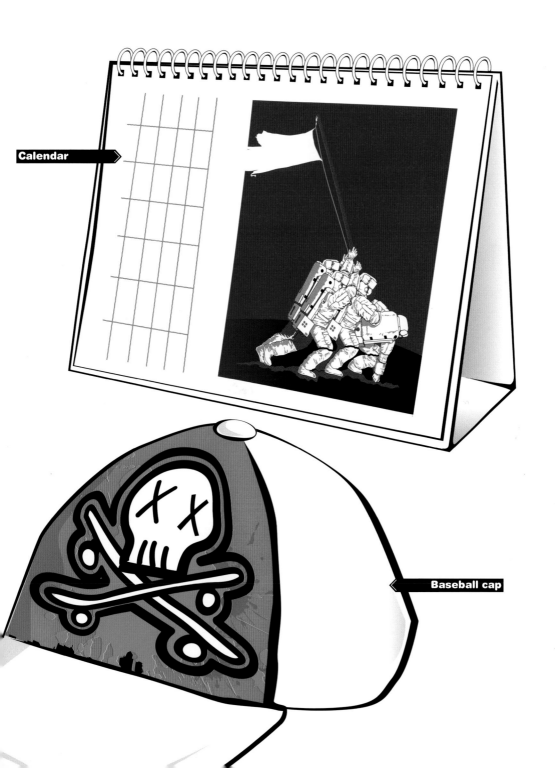

Calendar

Baseball cap

Origami

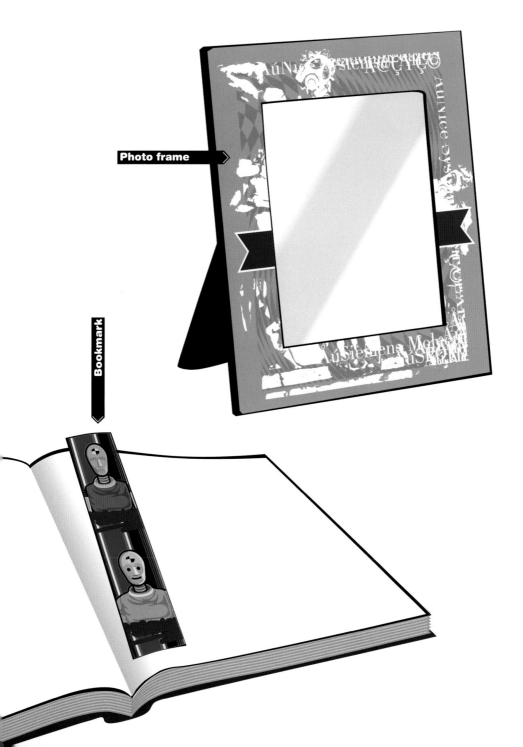

Photo frame

Bookmark

Coffee cup

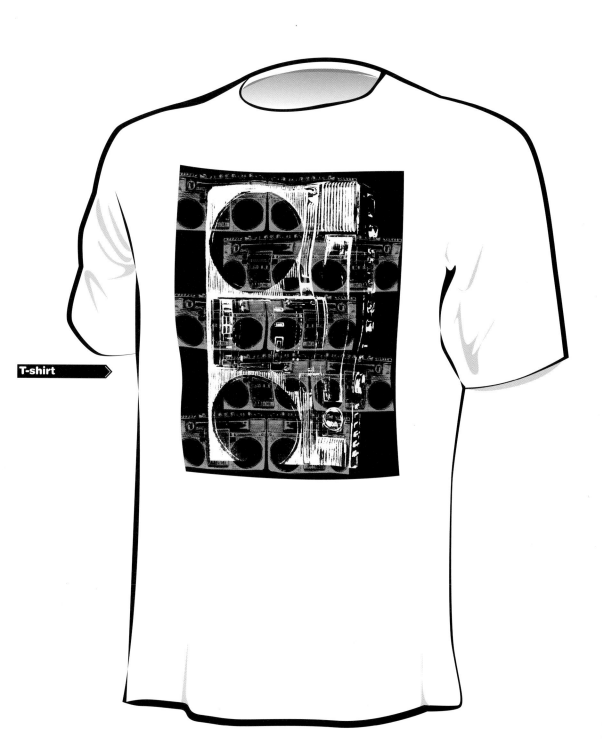

T-shirt

Wrapping paper

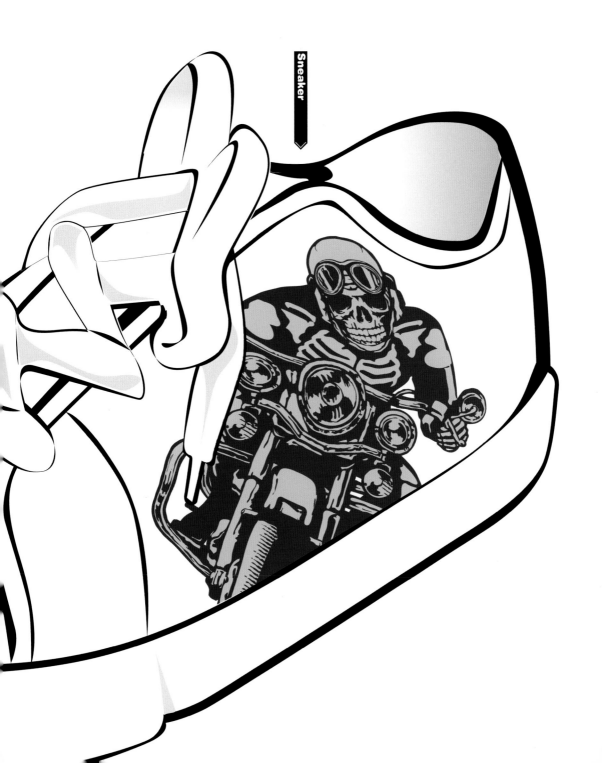

Sneaker

Lampshade

Greeting card

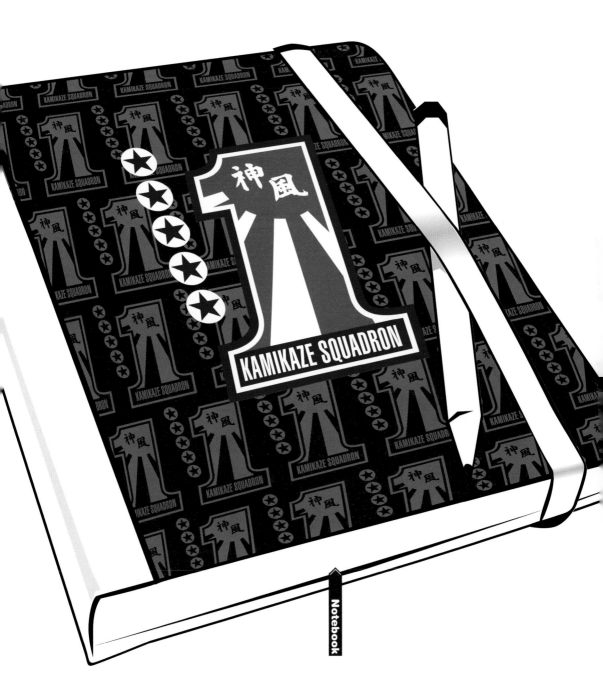

Umbrella

Dust jacket

Vase

Tote bag

TEMPLATES

SC_T26

TEMPLATES

SC_T36

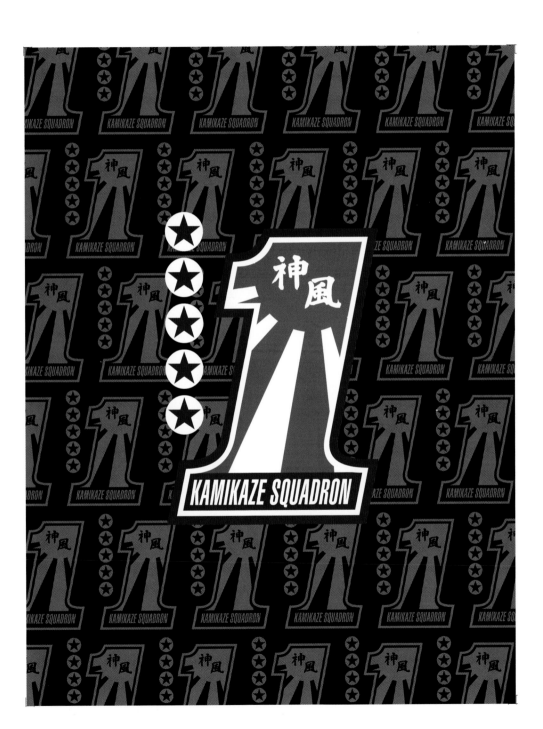

SC_T38

TEMPLATES

TEMPLATES

TEMPLATES

SC_T48

TEMPLATES

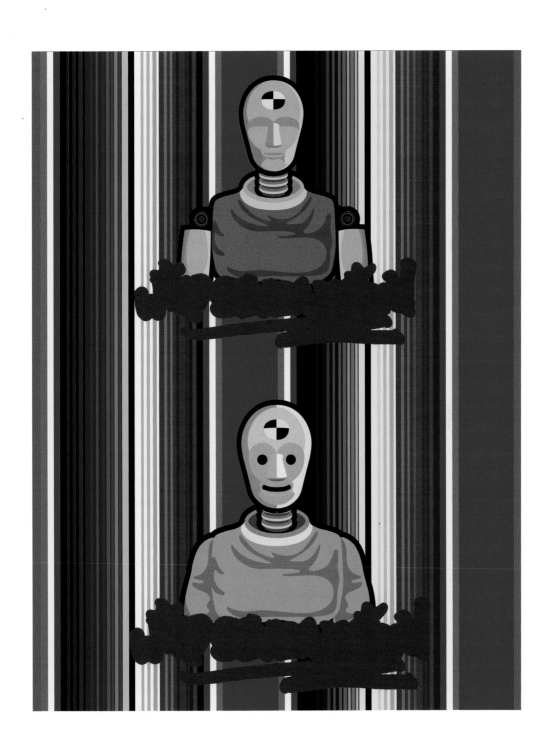

SC_T52   **TEMPLATES**

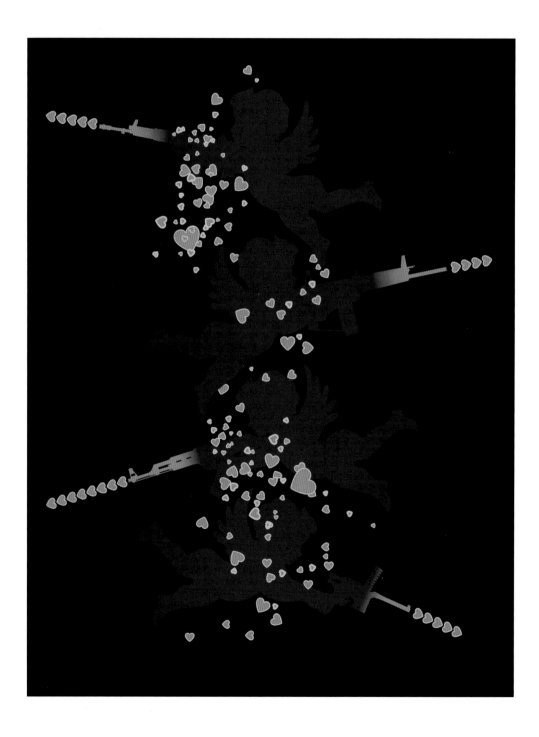

TEMPLATES

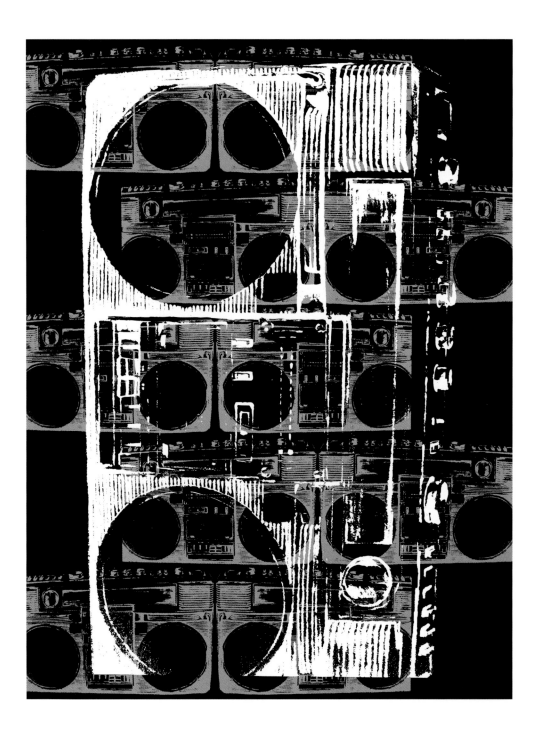

SC_T56

TEMPLATES

SC_T58

TEMPLATES

SC_T60

TEMPLATES

TEMPLATES

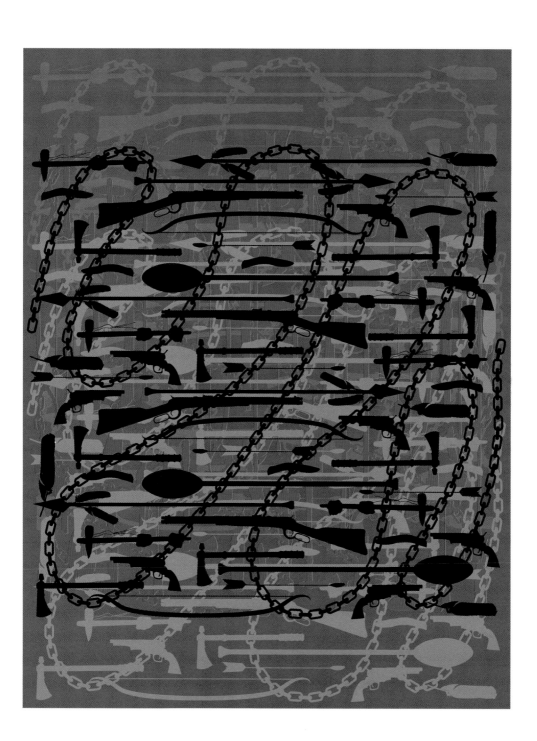

SC_T64   # TEMPLATES

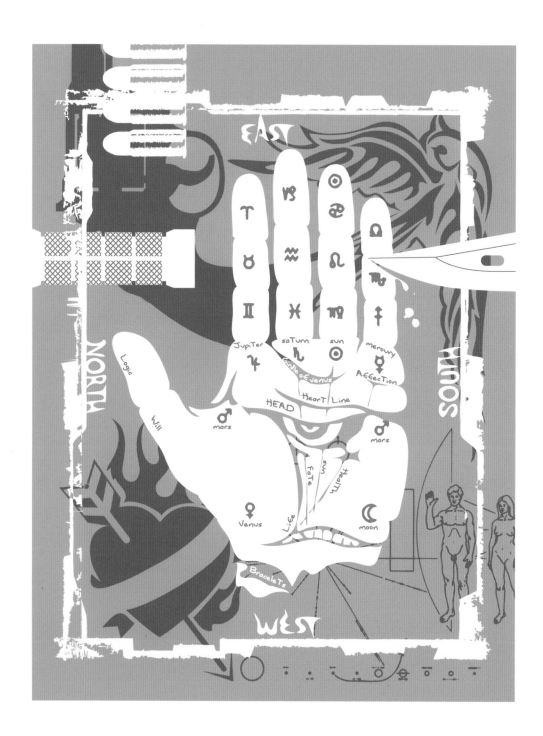

TEMPLATES

Incrociare
Le dita

TEMPLATES

TEMPLATES

SC_T76

TEMPLATES

TEMPLATES

SC_T82

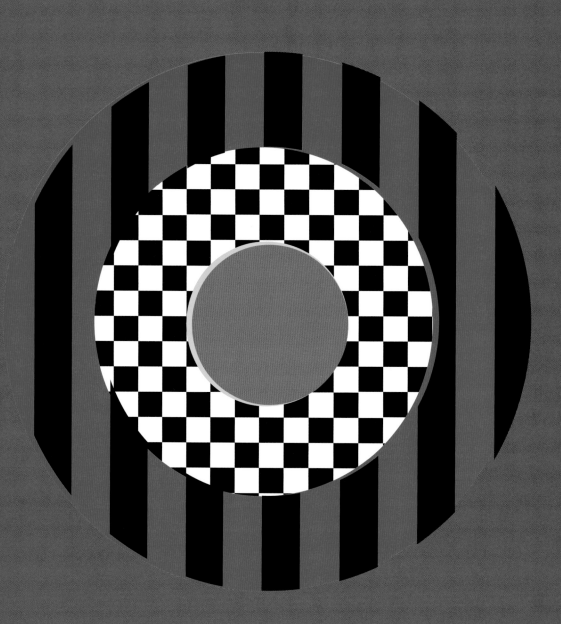

TEMPLATES

SC_T86

TEMPLATES

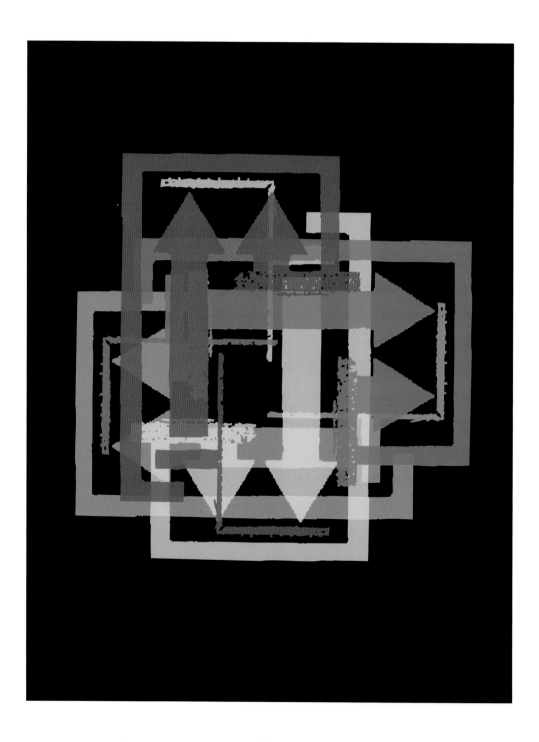

TEMPLATES

TEMPLATES

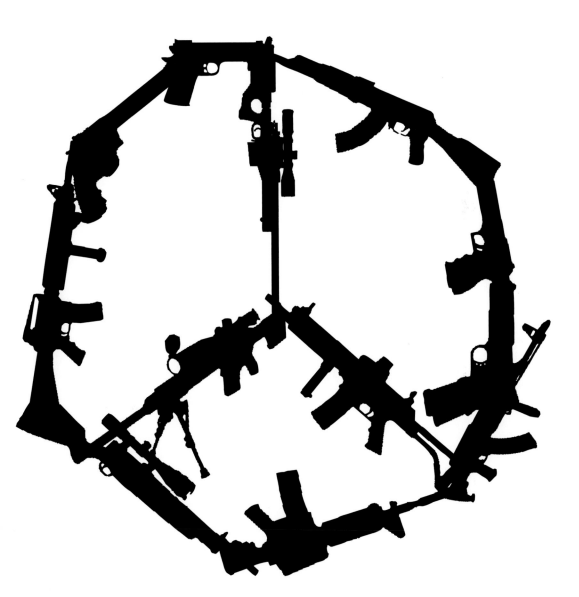

peace

SC_T94

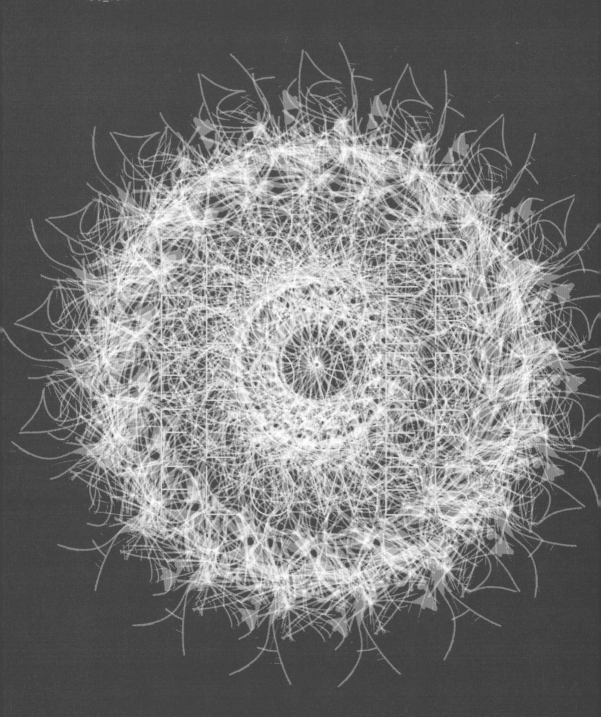

SC_T96   TEMPLATES

SC_T98

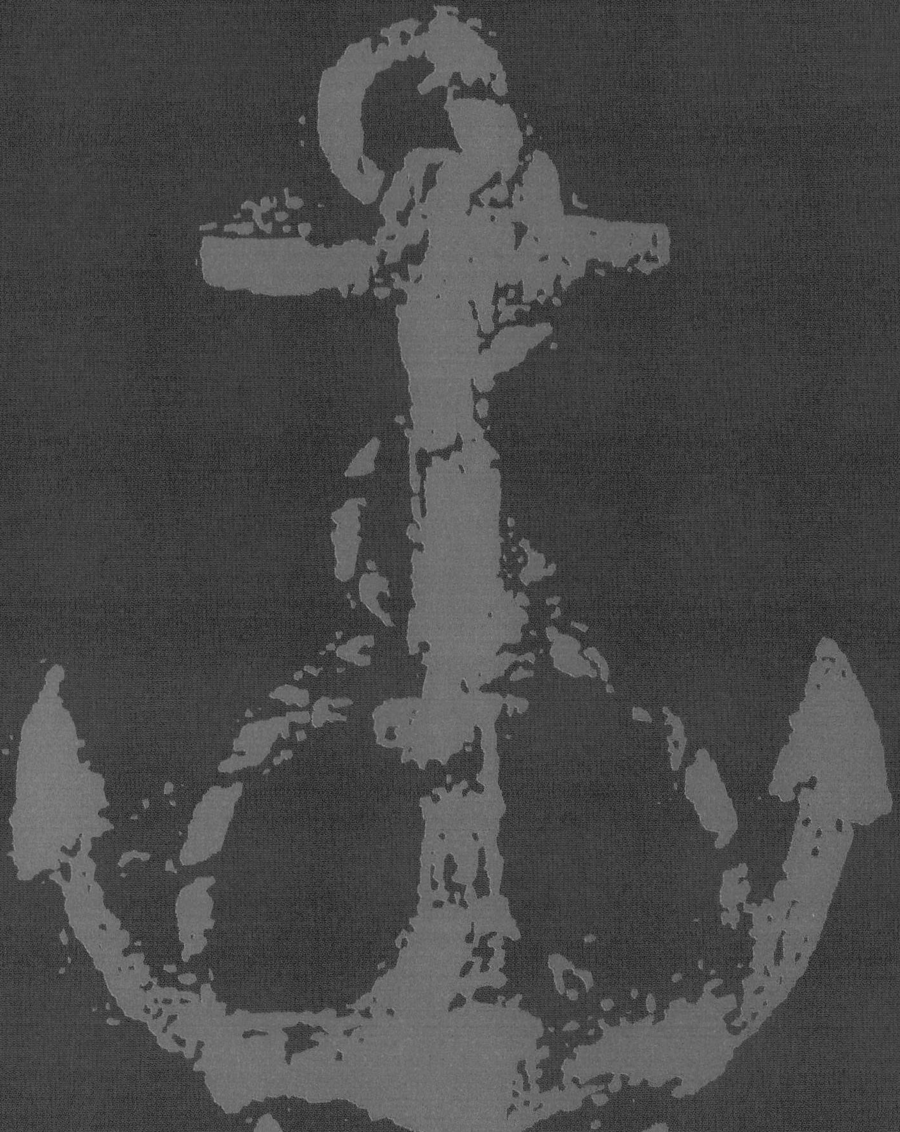

TEMPLATES

THINK
EARTh

COMPONENTS

COMPONENTS

From pages 26-27

File name: SC_T26_01
Page 26

File name: SC_T26_02
Page 26

File name: SC_T27_01
Page 27

File name: SC_T27_02
Page 27

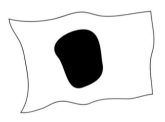

File name: SC_T27_03
Page 27

File name: SC_T27_04
Page 27

File name: SC_T27_05
Page 27

File name: SC_T27_06
Page 27

From pages 27-29

File name: SC_T27_07
Page 27

File name: SC_T28_01
Page 28

File name: SC_T28_02
Page 28

File name: SC_T28_03
Page 28

File name: SC_T29_01
Page 29

File name: SC_T29_02
Page 29

File name: SC_T29_03
Page 29

File name: SC_T29_04
Page 29

COMPONENTS

From pages 32-33

File name: SC_T29_05
Page 29

File name: SC_T32_01
Page 32

File name: SC_T32_02
Page 32

File name: SC_T32_03
Page 32

File name: SC_T32_04
Page 32

File name: SC_T32_05
Page 32

File name: SC_T33_01
Page 33

File name: SC_T33_02
Page 33

From pages 33-35

File name: SC_T33_03
Page 33

File name: SC_T34_01
Page 34

File name: SC_T34_02
Page 34

File name: SC_T34_03
Page 34

File name: SC_T35_01
Page 35

File name: SC_T35_02
Page 35

Golden Eagle

File name: SC_T35_03
Page 35

File name: SC_T35_04
Page 35

COMPONENTS

From pages 36-38

File name: SC_T36_01
Page 36

File name: SC_T37_01
Page 37

File name: SC_T37_02
Page 37

File name: SC_T37_03
Page 37

File name: SC_T37_04
Page 37

File name: SC_T37_05
Page 37

File name: SC_T38_01
Page 38

File name: SC_T38_02
Page 38

From page 38

File name: SC_T38_03
Page 38

File name: SC_T38_04
Page 38

File name: SC_T38_05
Page 38

File name: SC_T38_06
Page 38

File name: SC_T38_07
Page 38

File name: SC_T38_08
Page 38

File name: SC_T38_09
Page 38

File name: SC_T38_10
Page 38

COMPONENTS

From pages 38-42

File name: SC_T38_11
Page 38

File name: SC_T38_12
Page 38

File name: SC_T38_13
Page 38

File name: SC_T39_01
Page 39

File name: SC_T39_02
Page 39

File name: SC_T39_03
Page 39

File name: SC_T42_01
Page 42

File name: SC_T42_02
Page 42

From pages 42-44

File name: SC_T42_03
Page 42

File name: SC_T42_04
Page 42

File name: SC_T43_01
Page 43

File name: SC_T43_02
Page 43

File name: SC_T43_03
Page 43

File name: SC_T43_04
Page 43

File name: SC_T44_01
Page 44

File name: SC_T44_02
Page 44

COMPONENTS

From pages 45-47

File name: SC_T45_01
Page 45

File name: SC_T45_02
Page 45

File name: SC_T46_01
Page 46

File name: SC_T46_02
Page 46

File name: SC_T46_03
Page 46

File name: SC_T46_04
Page 46

File name: SC_T47_01
Page 47

File name: SC_T47_02
Page 47

From pages 47-52

File name: SC_T47_03
Page 47

File name: SC_T47_04
Page 47

File name: SC_T48_01
Page 48

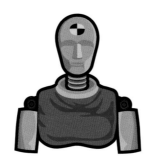

File name: SC_T49_01
Page 49

File name: SC_T49_02
Page 49

File name: SC_T49_03
Page 49

File name: SC_T52_01
Page 52

File name: SC_T52_02
Page 52

COMPONENTS

From pages 53-57

File name: SC_T53_01
Page 53

File name: SC_T54_01
Page 54

File name: SC_T55_01
Page 55

File name: SC_T55_02
Page 55

File name: SC_T55_03
Page 55

File name: SC_T56_01
Page 56

File name: SC_T57_01
Page 57

File name: SC_T57_02
Page 57

From pages 58-59

File name: SC_T58_01
Page 58

File name: SC_T58_02
Page 58

File name: SC_T58_03
Page 58

File name: SC_T58_04
Page 58

File name: SC_T58_05
Page 58

File name: SC_T59_01
Page 59

GLOBAL

File name: SC_T59_02
Page 59

File name: SC_T59_03
Page 59

COMPONENTS

From pages 59-61

File name: SC_T59_04
Page 59

File name: SC_T59_05
Page 59

File name: SC_T59_06
Page 59

File name: SC_T60_01
Page 60

File name: SC_T60_02
Page 60

File name: SC_T60_03
Page 60

File name: SC_T61_01
Page 61

File name: SC_T61_02
Page 61

From pages 62-63

File name: SC_T62_01
Page 62

File name: SC_T62_02
Page 62

File name: SC_T63_01
Page 63

File name: SC_T63_02
Page 63

File name: SC_T63_03
Page 63

File name: SC_T63_04
Page 63

File name: SC_T63_05
Page 63

File name: SC_T63_06
Page 63

COMPONENTS

From pages 63-64

File name: SC_T63_07
Page 63

File name: SC_T63_08
Page 63

File name: SC_T63_09
Page 63

File name: SC_T63_10
Page 63

File name: SC_T64_01
Page 64

File name: SC_T64_02
Page 64

File name: SC_T64_03
Page 64

File name: SC_T64_04
Page 64

From pages 65-66

File name: SC_T65_01
Page 65

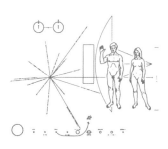

File name: SC_T65_02
Page 65

File name: SC_T65_03
Page 65

File name: SC_T66_01
Page 66

File name: SC_T66_02
Page 66

File name: SC_T66_03
Page 66

File name: SC_T66_04
Page 66

File name: SC_T66_05
Page 66

COMPONENTS

From page 67

File name: SC_T67_01
Page 67

File name: SC_T67_02
Page 67

File name: SC_T67_03
Page 67

File name: SC_T67_04
Page 67

File name: SC_T67_05
Page 67

File name: SC_T67_06
Page 67

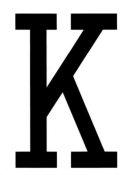

File name: SC_T67_07
Page 67

File name: SC_T67_08
Page 67

From pages 67-69

File name: SC_T67_09
Page 67

File name: SC_T67_10
Page 67

File name: SC_T67_11
Page 67

File name: SC_T68_01
Page 68

File name: SC_T68_02
Page 68

File name: SC_T68_03
Page 68

File name: SC_T69_01
Page 69

File name: SC_T69_02
Page 69

COMPONENTS

From pages 69-70

File name: SC_T69_03
Page 69

File name: SC_T69_04
Page 69

File name: SC_T69_05
Page 69

File name: SC_T69_06
Page 69

File name: SC_T70_01
Page 70

File name: SC_T70_02
Page 70

File name: SC_T70_03
Page 70

File name: SC_T70_04
Page 70

From pages 70-71

File name: SC_T70_05
Page 70

File name: SC_T71_01
Page 71

File name: SC_T71_02
Page 71

File name: SC_T71_03
Page 71

File name: SC_T71_04
Page 71

File name: SC_T71_05
Page 71

File name: SC_T71_06
Page 71

File name: SC_T71_07
Page 71

COMPONENTS

From pages 71-73

File name: SC_T71_08
Page 71

File name: SC_T71_09
Page 71

File name: SC_T71_10
Page 71

File name: SC_T72_01
Page 72

File name: SC_T72_02
Page 72

File name: SC_T72_03
Page 72

File name: SC_T72_04
Page 72

File name: SC_T73_01
Page 73

From pages 73-76

File name: SC_T73_02
Page 73

File name: SC_T73_03
Page 73

File name: SC_T73_04
Page 73

File name: SC_T73_05
Page 73

File name: SC_T76_01
Page 76

File name: SC_T76_02
Page 76

File name: SC_T76_03
Page 76

File name: SC_T76_04
Page 76

COMPONENTS

From pages 76-78

File name: SC_T76_05
Page 76

File name: SC_T76_06
Page 76

File name: SC_T77_01
Page 77

File name: SC_T77_02
Page 77

File name: SC_T77_03
Page 77

File name: SC_T77_04
Page 77

File name: SC_T78_01
Page 78

LOVE PEACE ECO

File name: SC_T78_02
Page 78

From pages 79-82

File name: SC_T79_01
Page 79

File name: SC_T79_02
Page 79

File name: SC_T80_01
Page 80

File name: SC_T80_02
Page 80

SPIDER

File name: SC_T80_03
Page 80

File name: SC_T81_01
Page 81

File name: SC_T82_01
Page 82

File name: SC_T82_02
Page 82

COMPONENTS

From pages 83-88

File name: SC_T83_01
Page 83

File name: SC_T84_01
Page 84

File name: SC_T84_02
Page 84

File name: SC_T85_01
Page 85

File name: SC_T85_02
Page 85

File name: SC_T86_01
Page 86

File name: SC_T87_01
Page 87

File name: SC_T88_01
Page 88

From pages 88-90

File name: SC_T88_02
Page 88

File name: SC_T88_03
Page 88

File name: SC_T88_04
Page 88

File name: SC_T89_01
Page 89

File name: SC_T89_02
Page 89

File name: SC_T89_03
Page 89

File name: SC_T90_01
Page 90

File name: SC_T90_02
Page 90

COMPONENTS

From pages 91-93

File name: SC_T91_01
Page 91

File name: SC_T91_02
Page 91

File name: SC_T92_01
Page 92

File name: SC_T92_02
Page 92

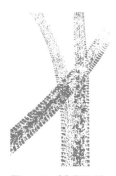

File name: SC_T92_03
Page 92

File name: SC_T93_01
Page 93

File name: SC_T93_02
Page 93

File name: SC_T93_03
Page 93

From pages 93-96

peace

File name: SC_T93_04
Page 93

File name: SC_T93_05
Page 93

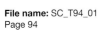
FLOWER

File name: SC_T94_01
Page 94

File name: SC_T94_02
Page 94

File name: SC_T95_01
Page 95

File name: SC_T96_01
Page 96

File name: SC_T96_02
Page 96

File name: SC_T96_03
Page 96

COMPONENTS

From pages 96-98

File name: SC_T96_04
Page 96

File name: SC_T97_01
Page 97

File name: SC_T97_02
Page 97

File name: SC_T97_03
Page 97

File name: SC_T97_04
Page 97

File name: SC_T97_05
Page 97

File name: SC_T97_06
Page 97

File name: SC_T98_01
Page 98

From pages 99-102

File name: SC_T99_01
Page 99

File name: SC_T99_02
Page 99

File name: SC_T99_03
Page 99

File name: SC_T100_01
Page 100

File name: SC_T100_02
Page 100

File name: SC_T101_01
Page 101

File name: SC_T101_02
Page 101

File name: SC_T102_01
Page 102

COMPONENTS

From pages 102-104

TODAY IS A GOOD DAY

File name: SC_T102_02
Page 102

File name: SC_T103_01
Page 103

File name: SC_T103_02
Page 103

File name: SC_T103_03
Page 103

File name: SC_T104_01
Page 104

File name: SC_T104_02
Page 104

File name: SC_T104_03
Page 104

File name: SC_T104_04
Page 104

From pages 105-107

File name: SC_T105_01
Page 105

File name: SC_T105_02
Page 105

File name: SC_T105_03
Page 105

File name: SC_T106_01
Page 106

File name: SC_T106_02
Page 106

File name: SC_T107_01
Page 107

File name: SC_T107_02
Page 107

License Agreement for the CD-ROM Files

Licenser: ricorico

1. License
Licenser hereby grants a non-exclusive and non-transferable right and license to use the Templates and Components files in the CD-ROM (hereinafter referred to as "Files") to a customer who purchased the book Bones and Skulls (hereinafter referred to as "Book"), and who agreed to the terms and conditions of this Agreement (hereinafter referred to as "User").

The User may process, modify, and/or edit the Files included in the CD-ROM or distribute them as a single file or in combination with other materials on a printed matter as design material in the User's work, such as:
    a. digital media, including websites.
    b. graphics for shop interiors and signs.
    c. leaflets, flyers, posters, direct mail, catalogues, pamphlets, and other tools for advertisement or sales promotion.
    d. goods, clothes, greeting cards, business cards, and other articles for personal production and use. The files may be used for personal, professional, and commercial purposes, provided that the articles produced are not offered for sale. The User may not sell articles made with the Files even when of a personal nature. Please read the following Limitations carefully:

2. Limitations
The User is not licensed to do any of the following:
    a. License, or otherwise by any means permit, any other person to use the Files.
    b. Use the Files for commercial production of postcards, business cards, or any other articles, or sell any such articles made using the Files.
    c. Provide downloading services using the Files (including greeting card services).
    d. Use the Files in order to produce any software or any other objects for sale.
    e. Acquire the copyright in any material in the Files or any objects created using the Files.
    f. Use the Files to create obscene, scandalous, abusive or slanderous works.

3. Copyright and Other Intellectual Property
ricorico and its suppliers reserve the copyright and other intellectual property rights in the Files. When specifying the User of a product made using the Files, please also indicate "© 2010 ricorico".

4. Exclusion of Damages
In no event shall Rockport Publishers and ricorico be liable for any damages whatsoever (including but not limited to, damages for loss of profit or loss of the file contents) related to the use or inability to use the Files or use the materials in the Files.

5. Termination of this License Agreement
If the User breaches any of the articles in this Agreement, Rockport Publishers and ricorico have the right to withdraw the User's License granted on the basis hereof.

ABOUT THE AUTHOR

ricoricio *is a Tokyo-based book packaging company established in 2009. They have been actively producing books in the area of graphic design, photography, craft, pop culture, and manga, including two titles that they also authored.*